Make Room

A CHILD'S GUIDE TO LENT AND EASTER

Laura Alary

Illustrated by Ann Boyajian

PARACLETE PRESS

BREWSTER, MASSACHUSETTS

For Iain, Maggie and Miriam, my companions on the journey
—L.A.

For Winona and Delila, my muses and willing models
—A.B.

2019 Third Printing
2017 Second Printing
2016 First Printing

Make Room: A Child's Guide to Lent and Easter

Text Copyright © 2016 by Laura Alary
Illustrations Copyright © 2016 by Ann Boyajian

ISBN 978-1-61261-659-9

The Paraclete Press name and logo (dove on cross) are trademarks of Paraclete Press, Inc.

Library of Congress Cataloging-in-Publication Data
Names: Alary, Laura. | Boyajian, Ann, illustrator.
Title: Make room : a child's guide to Lent and Easter / Laura Alary ;
   illustrated by Ann Boyajian.
Description: Brewster MA : Paraclete Press Inc., 2016.
Identifiers: LCCN 2015040585 | ISBN 9781612616599
Subjects: LCSH: Lent—Juvenile literature. | Easter—Juvenile literature.
Classification: LCC BV85 .A43 2016 | DDC 263/.92—dc23
LC record available at http://lccn.loc.gov/2015040585

10 9 8 7 6 5 4 3

Published by Paraclete Press
Brewster, Massachusetts
www.paracletepress.com

Printed in the United States of America

This is the Season of Lent.
The church is dressed in purple.

The world outside has its own seasons and its own colors.
These days we are in the gray time between winter and spring.
Some mornings the puddles are frozen hard
    and the bare branches of trees scrape a snow-white sky.
Other days the air is warmer, ice is melting,
    and the air smells faintly of damp earth and rotting leaves.
Under the ground seeds and bulbs are sleeping,
    dreaming in shades of green.
We are all waiting for spring.

In church we are waiting too, waiting for Easter.
While we wait, we get ready.

Making Time

Long ago, Jesus went out alone into the desert to get ready.
Deep inside he felt that God had important work for him to do.
But he needed help to see clearly the way ahead.
For forty days and forty nights he was in the desert by himself,

Wondering
Talking with God
Listening
Making choices.

I wonder why Jesus went into the desert?
Maybe it was quiet and still.
Maybe Jesus thought he could hear God better there.
Maybe he needed to make time to listen
  so he would know which way to go.

During Lent we make time to be with God.

Every day we talk with God in different ways.

Sometimes we pray with words.

Sometimes we sing or listen to music.

Sometimes we get out paints and crayons and create many-colored prayers.

Colors are like a different language we can all speak
   even when we have no words.

God understands.

At other times we make silence.

We turn off the television and the music
   and stop talking for a while.

Then we practice listening.

Sometimes we read stories from the Bible
   and we wonder about what God might be telling us.

Sometimes we just sit and rest in the quiet.

During Lent we pay attention to how we live.

We think about the choices we make every day.

We ask hard questions:

   Does what we say and do make the world a better place?

   Or not?

   Does how we live make God happy?

   Or sad?

   Is there anything we need to change?

Lent lasts for forty days and forty nights,
   plus six Sundays.

We count the days by snuffing out purple candles,
   one for each week.

Forty days is a long time.

But it takes time to get ready.

Making Space

After Jesus came back from the desert
   he left everything behind.
Trusting God to give him what he needed,
   he began to travel from place to place
   telling everyone who would listen
   about God and the Kingdom of God.

The Kingdom of God is the world
   the way God imagined it in the very beginning,
   the way God wants it to be.

Many people came to hear Jesus.
They were full of questions:
What is the Kingdom of God? Where is it? How do we get there?

Jesus told them:

The Kingdom of God is like a tiny mustard seed

that grows into a huge plant,

so big and strong that birds can build nests in it.

The Kingdom of God is like a pinch of yeast

stirred into a big mixing bowl of flour.

It is only a speck, but it makes a big batch of dough rise.

The Kingdom of God is inside you.

But it needs time and space to grow.

This is how to make space:
    If you have done wrong,
      tell God you are sorry.
    Sweep your heart clean and start fresh.

Be kind to all people,
    not just the ones who like you.
Open your heart wide.

If someone hurts you
    ask God to help you forgive.
Do not store up angry thoughts.
Let them go.

Make space inside for better things.
Share so that everyone has enough.
If you have two coats
    give one to someone who has none.
Why clutter up your life with more than you can use?
Make space for what really matters.

One day when his friends wanted to learn to talk with God
　　Jesus taught them to pray this way:

> *Our Father who art in heaven,*
>
> 　　*hallowed be thy name.*
>
> *Thy kingdom come.*
>
> *Thy will be done,*
>
> 　　*on earth as it is in heaven.*
>
> *Give us this day our daily bread.*
>
> *And forgive us our trespasses,*
>
> 　　*as we forgive those who trespass against us.*
>
> *And lead us not into temptation,*
>
> 　　*but deliver us from evil.*

When we pray for the Kingdom of God to come
we are telling God what we hope for.
We hope that people everywhere will listen for God,
　　live the way God wants,
　　　　and make space for what really matters.
　　　　　　　　　Imagine.

16

During Lent we make space.

We clean our whole house.

We sort our clothes and toys and books
   and give away what we do not use.

It is hard at first.

I like my things and I want to keep all of them.

But someone else might need them more than I do.

Besides, I like having space in my room.

It makes me feel lighter.

During Lent we think about the Kingdom of God.
We plant seeds and wait for them to sprout.
We mix yeast into water and flour and watch the dough rise.
When the dough has risen,
    we roll and twist it to make pretzels.
They look like little arms crossed in prayer.

At supper we cross our arms this way
   and pray that the Kingdom of God will come.
I wonder how this will happen?
Maybe the Kingdom of God starts very small
   but grows bigger and bigger
   so slowly we hardly notice.
Maybe the Kingdom of God happens right around us.
Maybe it is happening now.

During Lent we make our lives more simple.

We eat plain meals, sometimes just bread and soup.

Everyone helps with the cooking.

We even give up buying some of our favorite treats and snacks.

Instead we put the money in a jar and save it.

When Lent is over we will buy groceries for the food bank.

Making do with less means that someone else can have enough.

That seems fair.

I like to have nice things. I like to buy treats.

And I like to eat my favorite foods.

But not all the time.

There are times for filling up and times for emptying out.

Lent is a time for emptying,

　　for sharing, for giving away. It is good to make space.

Making Room

Wherever Jesus went, people wanted to be near him.

Some were sick and hoped Jesus could make them better.

Some had questions and hoped Jesus could give them answers.

Some felt dirty because they had done bad things.

They hoped Jesus could make them clean.

Some were hungry and wanted food.

Some were lonely and wanted company.

Some were angry at the unfairness of the world
   and hoped Jesus could set things right.

So many people needed so many things.

Sometimes Jesus got very tired.

But he never turned anyone away.

His friends worried about him.

They tried to help him rest.

They shooed away the children.

They tried to send the crowds home.

But Jesus said:

Let them come! Everyone is welcome.
The Kingdom of God is like a great feast.
All kinds of people will come to it
from every place and time.

Some people did not like the way Jesus made room.

Look at him, they said.

He chooses the wrong friends.

He should know better.

He cannot be a good man
   if he spends time with bad people.

But Jesus kept inviting people in.

Through what he said and what he did he sent this
message:

We can always make the circle bigger.
There is room for all around God's table.

During Lent we make room.

We invite a neighbor to our house to share our soup.

We make cards and decorate them,
   then send them to people who are sad or sick or alone.

We try hard to see people the way Jesus saw them.

After church on Sunday when we have juice and cookies
   lots of friends stand together in tight little circles.

A few strangers stand alone by the wall.

I wonder how we can make room for them.

Maybe I can start by smiling and saying hello.

I think Jesus would like that.

Holy Week

The last week in Lent is called Holy Week.
Holy Week is filled with stories about Jesus.

On Palm Sunday we hear how Jesus and his friends
    traveled to the great city of Jerusalem
    to celebrate the feast of the Passover.
At Passover the people of God remember
    that they were once slaves in Egypt.
They remember how God saved them.
They remember how God led them through the sea
        and the desert to freedom.

As Jesus came near Jerusalem,
    crowds of people welcomed him.
They threw their coats and palm branches on the road
    and shouted "Hosanna!" "Save us now!"
I wonder who they thought Jesus was?
I wonder what they hoped he would do for them?

On Maundy Thursday we bring soup and bread to church and eat together.

After supper we go into the sanctuary.

We hear the story of the night Jesus and his friends
   ate together for the last time.

Before the meal Jesus took a cloth, a bowl, and a pitcher of water.

He got down on his knees and washed his friends' feet,
   which were dirty and sore from walking.

That is who Jesus is.

He pours himself out like water from a pitcher.

He touches what is dirty and hurting and makes it clean and whole.

Jesus told his friends:

> *This is what you must do for each other.*
>
> *Love one another as I have loved you.*

On Friday we come to church again.
We hear how people who did not like Jesus came
    and carried him away.
They made fun of him, bullied him, hurt him.
They took everything from him, even his clothes.
They nailed him to a cross.
Jesus died.

As we listen to this story
    everything around us changes.
The candles on the altar are snuffed out one by one.
Darkness creeps in.
All the colors are carried away.
The cross is draped in black.
The church is not dressed in purple anymore.
It is bare and sad and full of shadows.
Outside on the street I hear people laughing and talking.
It seems wrong.
Don't they know what has happened to Jesus?

But then, on Sunday we get up while it is still dark.

We walk to the lake and meet other people from our church.

Wrapped in blankets, we shiver in the cold and wait.

A streak of pink appears in the sky, then the sun, huge and blazing orange.

The darkness drains away and even the air feels full to the brim with color.

God has done a wonderful thing.

"Hallelujah!" we sing.
"Jesus is risen!"
"The Lord is risen indeed!"
The colors of the sunrise spill over
   and splash into our church.
Everywhere there are flowers
   and green leaves,
beautiful banners and bright sunlight.
The shadows are gone.
Lent is over.

We have made time.
We have made space.
We have made room.
We are ready now.
We are different.
Everything is different.
The whole world is new!
It is Easter morning!